BOOK of SPACE
Questions and Answers

By Rosie McCormick

Contents

Introduction — 3

Space — 4

Stars — 6

The Sun — 10

The Moon — 12

Our Solar System — 16

Exploring Space — 20

Key Events in Space Exploration — 24

Introduction

What do you want to know about space?

People have always asked questions about space. You can find answers to some of your questions in this book. Scientists have found many answers to their questions by using telescopes, spacecraft, and other tools. They have made amazing discoveries, but there is still much more to explore.

Space

What makes up space?

When you look up at the night sky, you are looking at space. Space is filled with many things, including planets, moons, stars, and other objects. A star is a ball of gas that gives off light and heat. A planet is a large object that moves around a star. A moon is an object that moves around a planet.

What is our place in space?

We live on a planet called Earth. Earth moves around the Sun, which is a star. Many objects move around the Sun, including eight major planets. Earth is the third planet from the Sun.

Earth

Stars

What makes the stars shine?

Stars are huge balls of gas. They produce heat and light. Most stars look like bright dots because they are so far away. We cannot see their real colors. Very hot stars are blue. Medium-hot stars are yellow. The coolest stars are red.

The brightness of a star depends on how much light it produces. The hotter a star is, the more brightly it shines. Large stars are usually brighter than small stars. The closer a star is to Earth, the brighter it appears to us.

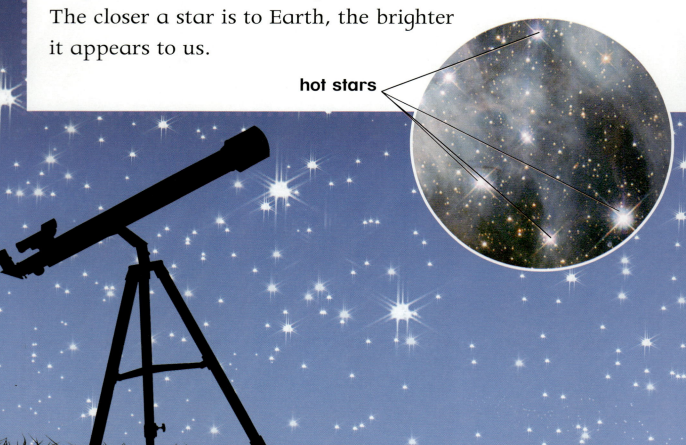

hot stars

Why do we only see most stars at night?

The Sun is the closest star to Earth. It is so close that it appears very bright. During the day the Sun is so bright that we usually cannot see other stars. Even though we cannot see the other stars and planets during the daytime, they are still in space.

What are constellations?

Sometimes people imagine that the stars form pictures in the sky. Sometimes they see the shapes of animals, objects, and people. Constellations are the groups of stars that form these pictures. Long ago some people gave the star pictures names such as the Lion, the Scorpion, and the Southern Cross. There are eighty-eight constellations that we can see in the entire sky.

Scorpion

Southern Cross

Lion

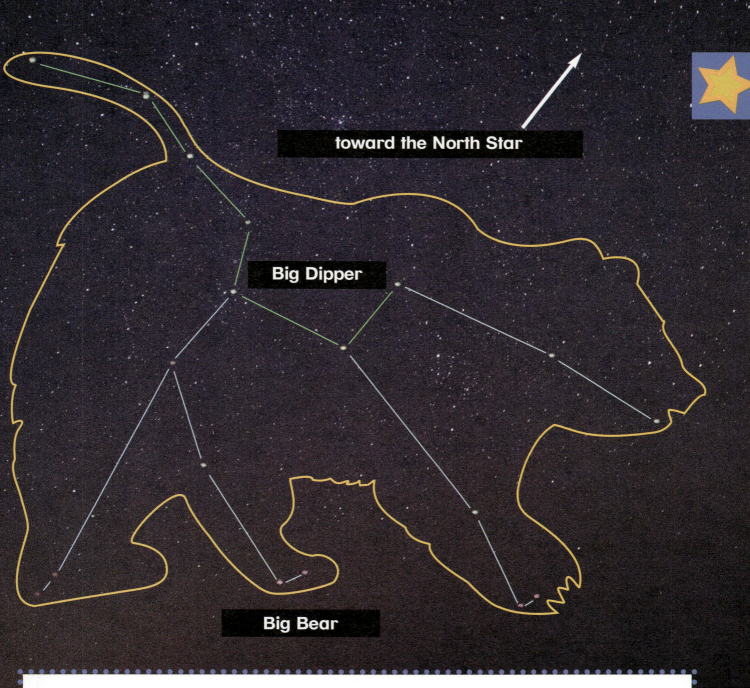

How do star watchers use constellations?

Star gazers use constellations to find individual stars. For example, one constellation is called the Big Bear. It contains a smaller group of seven stars called the Big Dipper. Two bright stars in the Big Dipper help you find the North Star. Sometimes when people are lost, they use the North Star to guide them.

The Sun

What kind of star is the Sun?

The Sun is a yellow star. The temperature of the center of the Sun is more than 25 million degrees Fahrenheit. For a star, that is only medium-hot. The Sun is much bigger than Earth. More than a million Earths could fit inside our Sun. Compared to other stars, however, the Sun is medium-sized.

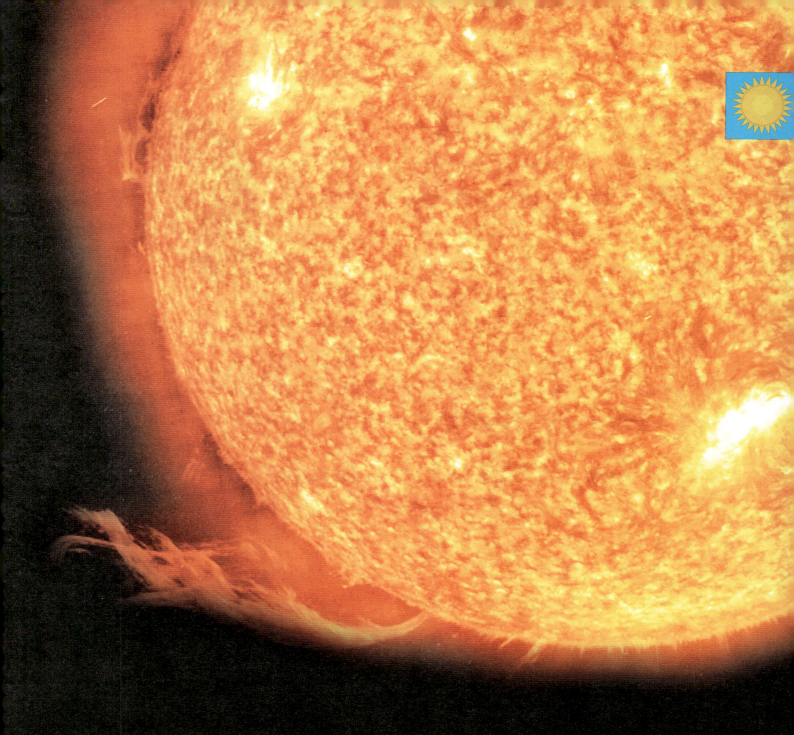

How far away is the Sun?

The Sun is about 93 million miles from Earth. If Earth were closer to the Sun, it would be too hot for people to live on our planet. If it were much farther away, it would be too cold.

The Moon

What is it like on the Moon?

The Moon is an object that moves around Earth. Like Earth, the Moon has rocks and soil. The surface of the Moon has many holes. These holes are called craters. There are also mountains on the Moon. On parts of the Moon the temperature is hotter than boiling water. On other parts it is colder than ice.

Can people live on the Moon?

People cannot live on the Moon today. Plants and animals need air to breathe and water to drink. There is no air or water on the Moon. To live on the Moon, people must bring air and water with them.

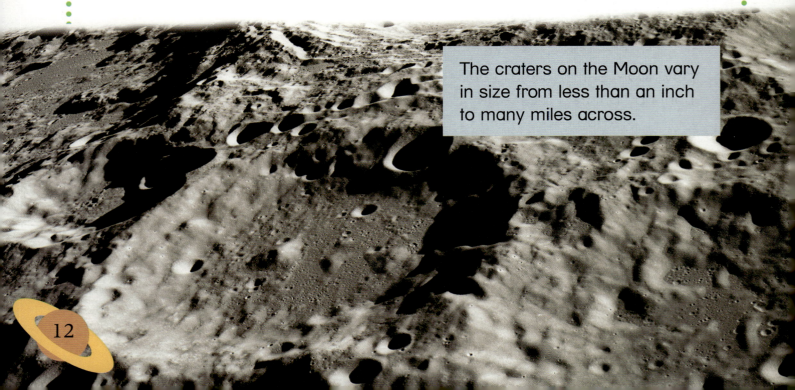

The craters on the Moon vary in size from less than an inch to many miles across.

How far away is the Moon?

The Moon is about 238,000 miles from Earth. If you could drive to the Moon, it would take months to get there. If you traveled by a spacecraft, it would take a few days. The Moon is our closest neighbor in space.

Moon

Earth

How does the Moon shine?

Even though the Moon shines, it has no light of its own. The light from the Moon comes from the Sun. The Sun shines on the Moon just like it shines on Earth. People see the part of the Moon that has the Sun's light shining on it.

Why does the Moon seem to change shape?

The Moon travels around Earth. As the Moon moves, only the surface that is lighted by the Sun can be seen on Earth. This makes it look like the Moon changes shape. The Moon does not change shape. It is always a sphere, like the shape of a ball.

full Moon

quarter Moon

crescent Moon

Our Solar System

What is our solar system?

Our solar system is made up of the Sun and the objects that move around it. There are eight major planets in our solar system. Many of them have moons. There are more than one hundred moons in all. There are also millions of smaller objects in our solar system such as asteroids and comets. Scientists discover new objects in our solar system all the time.

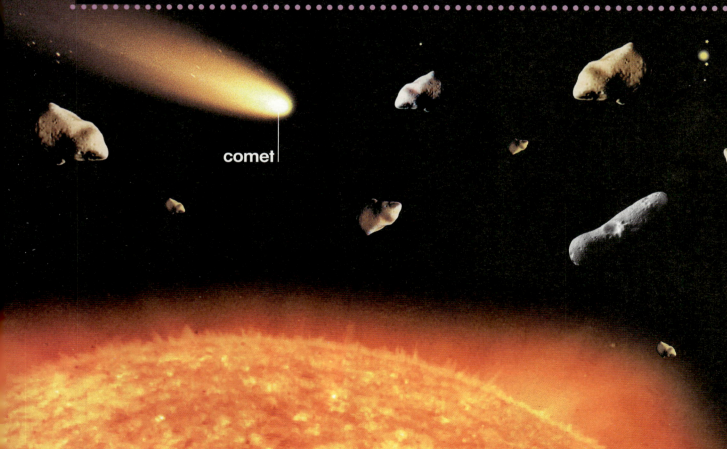

comet

What is an orbit?

An orbit is the path an object takes when it travels around something. When we say a planet "orbits" the Sun, we mean it follows a path around the Sun. All the planets in our solar system orbit the Sun. The Moon orbits Earth. Other moons orbit other planets.

What are the planets in our solar system?

The eight major planets in our solar system are Mercury, Venus, Earth, Mars, Jupiter, Saturn, Uranus, and Neptune. Mercury is the smallest and Jupiter is the biggest of these planets.

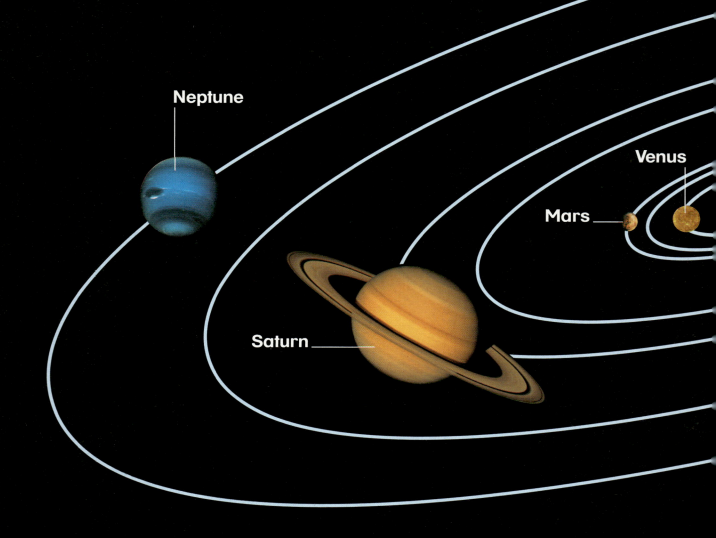

This diagram shows how the major planets in our solar system orbit the Sun.

Exploring Space

How do people explore space?

Long ago people explored space by looking at the night sky. Today scientists still do this, but they use telescopes to help them see more clearly. Astronauts and machines called space probes also explore space.

These telescopes on Mauna Kea, Hawaii, take pictures of space objects.

What do telescopes do?

People use telescopes to study space. Telescopes make distant objects appear larger and brighter. They allow people to see far into space more clearly. Some telescopes are used to take pictures of planets and stars.

Today scientists use computers to control most telescopes. Some telescopes are on Earth. Others, like the Hubble Space Telescope, are in space.

Hubble Space Telescope

What are space probes?

Space probes are machines that study space. The machines go to faraway planets and moons. Probes collect information and take close-up pictures that a telescope on Earth could not take.

One space probe scientists have used is called *Galileo*. The space probe took pictures of volcanoes erupting on one of Jupiter's moons. It sent the information and pictures back to scientists on Earth.

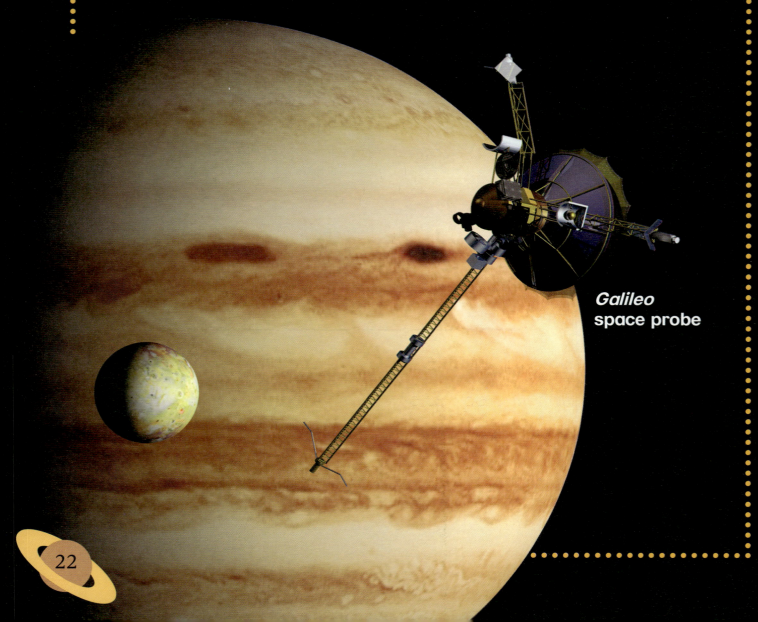

Galileo space probe

What do astronauts do?

Astronauts make new discoveries each time they travel into space. Sometimes they repair equipment in space. Some astronauts live aboard space stations. The experiments they carry out help others learn more about space and about Earth.

astronauts working in space

Key Events in Space Exploration

1957  *Sputnik I* is launched. It is the first object made by humans to orbit the Earth.

1959  *Luna 2* is the first spacecraft to land on the Moon.

1961 Cosmonaut Yuri Gagarin is the first person to travel in space. He journeys once around Earth on April 12, in a flight lasting 108 minutes.

1968 *Apollo 8* is the first spacecraft to fly with people around the Moon and return to Earth.

1969 On the *Apollo 11* mission, astronaut Neil Armstrong is the first person to walk on the Moon on July 20.

1981 The Space Shuttle *Columbia* was sent into orbit around Earth. It is the first spacecraft that could be reused in space.

1990 The Space Shuttle *Discovery* releases the Hubble Space Telescope. Its purpose is to study objects in space.

2000 The International Space Station opens in November. Astronauts and scientists from many nations live and work on the space station. They study what it is like to live in space.

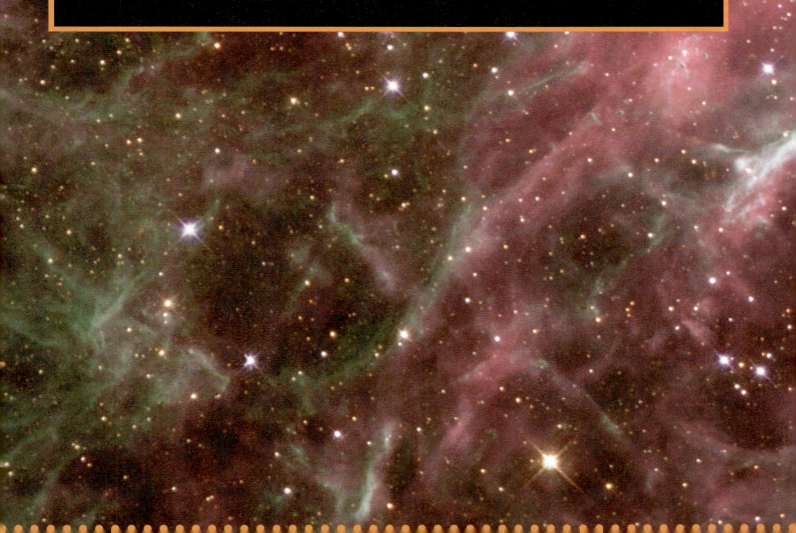

BOOK of SPACE
Questions and Answers

By Rosie McCormick

Contents

Introduction 3

Space 4

Stars 6

The Sun 10

The Moon 12

Our Solar System 16

Exploring Space 20

Key Events in Space Exploration 24

Introduction

What do you want to know about space?

People have always asked questions about space. You can find answers to some of your questions in this book. Scientists have found many answers to their questions by using telescopes, spacecraft, and other tools. They have made amazing discoveries, but there is still much more to explore.

Space

What makes up space?

When you look up at the night sky, you are looking at space. Space is filled with many things, including planets, moons, stars, and other objects. A star is a ball of gas that gives off light and heat. A planet is a large object that moves around a star. A moon is an object that moves around a planet.

What is our place in space?

We live on a planet called Earth. Earth moves around the Sun, which is a star. Many objects move around the Sun, including eight major planets. Earth is the third planet from the Sun.

Earth

Stars

What makes the stars shine?

Stars are huge balls of gas. They produce heat and light. Most stars look like bright dots because they are so far away. We cannot see their real colors. Very hot stars are blue. Medium-hot stars are yellow. The coolest stars are red.

The brightness of a star depends on how much light it produces. The hotter a star is, the more brightly it shines. Large stars are usually brighter than small stars. The closer a star is to Earth, the brighter it appears to us.

hot stars

Why do we only see most stars at night?

The Sun is the closest star to Earth. It is so close that it appears very bright. During the day the Sun is so bright that we usually cannot see other stars. Even though we cannot see the other stars and planets during the daytime, they are still in space.

What are constellations?

Sometimes people imagine that the stars form pictures in the sky. Sometimes they see the shapes of animals, objects, and people. Constellations are the groups of stars that form these pictures. Long ago some people gave the star pictures names such as the Lion, the Scorpion, and the Southern Cross. There are eighty-eight constellations that we can see in the entire sky.

Scorpion

Southern Cross

Lion

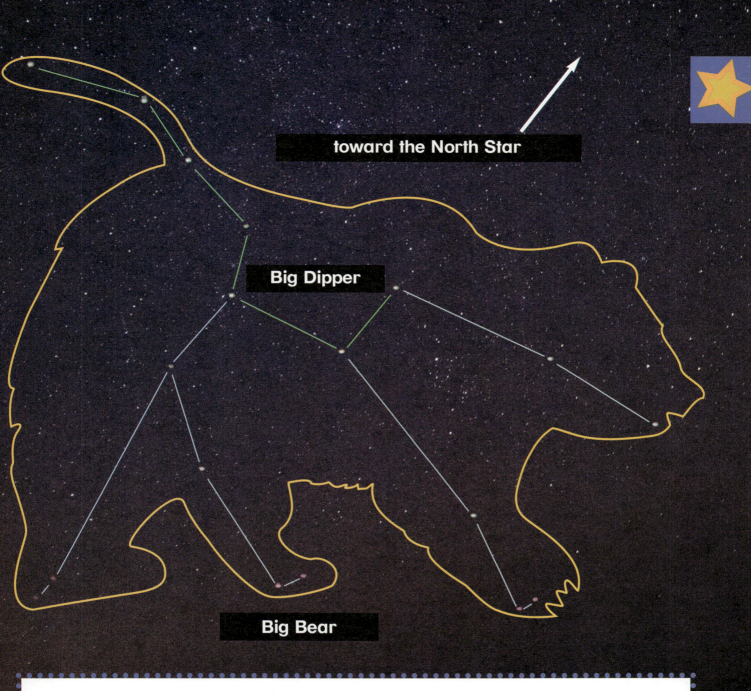

How do star watchers use constellations?

Star gazers use constellations to find individual stars. For example, one constellation is called the Big Bear. It contains a smaller group of seven stars called the Big Dipper. Two bright stars in the Big Dipper help you find the North Star. Sometimes when people are lost, they use the North Star to guide them.

The Sun

What kind of star is the Sun?

The Sun is a yellow star. The temperature of the center of the Sun is more than 25 million degrees Fahrenheit. For a star, that is only medium-hot. The Sun is much bigger than Earth. More than a million Earths could fit inside our Sun. Compared to other stars, however, the Sun is medium-sized.

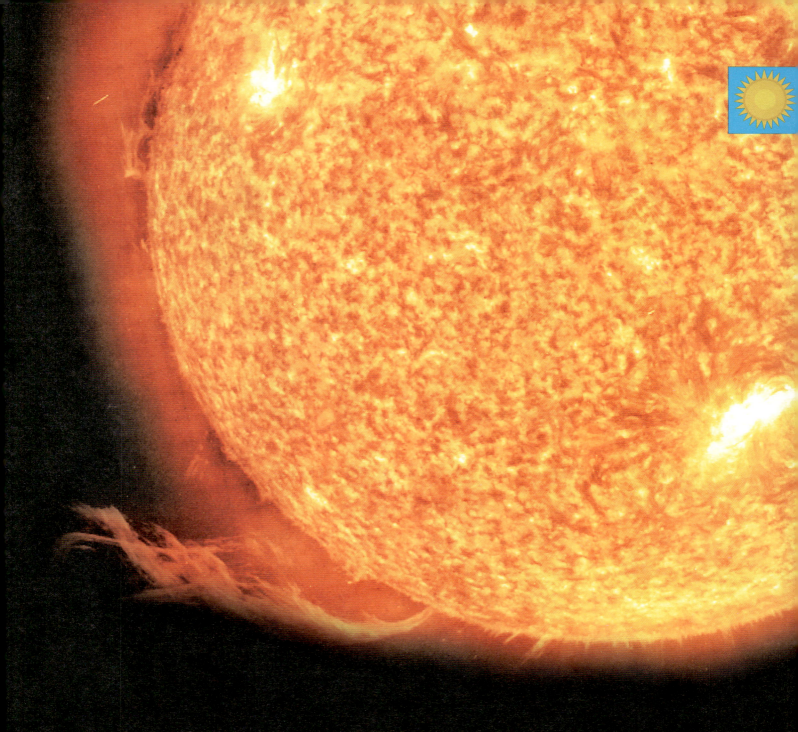

How far away is the Sun?

The Sun is about 93 million miles from Earth. If Earth were closer to the Sun, it would be too hot for people to live on our planet. If it were much farther away, it would be too cold.

The Moon

What is it like on the Moon?

The Moon is an object that moves around Earth. Like Earth, the Moon has rocks and soil. The surface of the Moon has many holes. These holes are called craters. There are also mountains on the Moon. On parts of the Moon the temperature is hotter than boiling water. On other parts it is colder than ice.

Can people live on the Moon?

People cannot live on the Moon today. Plants and animals need air to breathe and water to drink. There is no air or water on the Moon. To live on the Moon, people must bring air and water with them.

The craters on the Moon vary in size from less than an inch to many miles across.

How far away is the Moon?

The Moon is about 238,000 miles from Earth. If you could drive to the Moon, it would take months to get there. If you traveled by a spacecraft, it would take a few days. The Moon is our closest neighbor in space.

Moon

Earth

How does the Moon shine?

Even though the Moon shines, it has no light of its own. The light from the Moon comes from the Sun. The Sun shines on the Moon just like it shines on Earth. People see the part of the Moon that has the Sun's light shining on it.

Why does the Moon seem to change shape?

The Moon travels around Earth. As the Moon moves, only the surface that is lighted by the Sun can be seen on Earth. This makes it look like the Moon changes shape. The Moon does not change shape. It is always a sphere, like the shape of a ball.

full Moon

quarter Moon

crescent Moon

Our Solar System

What is our solar system?

Our solar system is made up of the Sun and the objects that move around it. There are eight major planets in our solar system. Many of them have moons. There are more than one hundred moons in all. There are also millions of smaller objects in our solar system such as asteroids and comets. Scientists discover new objects in our solar system all the time.

comet

What is an orbit?

An orbit is the path an object takes when it travels around something. When we say a planet "orbits" the Sun, we mean it follows a path around the Sun. All the planets in our solar system orbit the Sun. The Moon orbits Earth. Other moons orbit other planets.

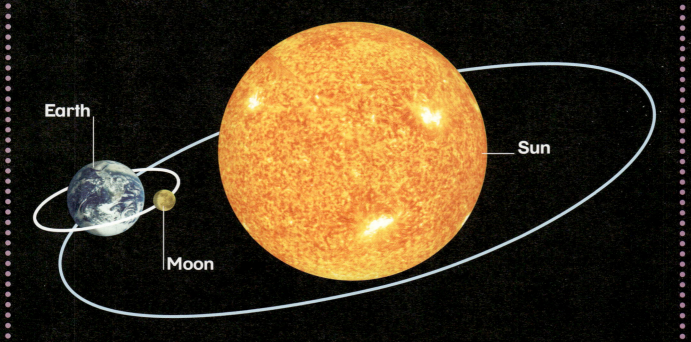

What are the planets in our solar system?

The eight major planets in our solar system are Mercury, Venus, Earth, Mars, Jupiter, Saturn, Uranus, and Neptune. Mercury is the smallest and Jupiter is the biggest of these planets.

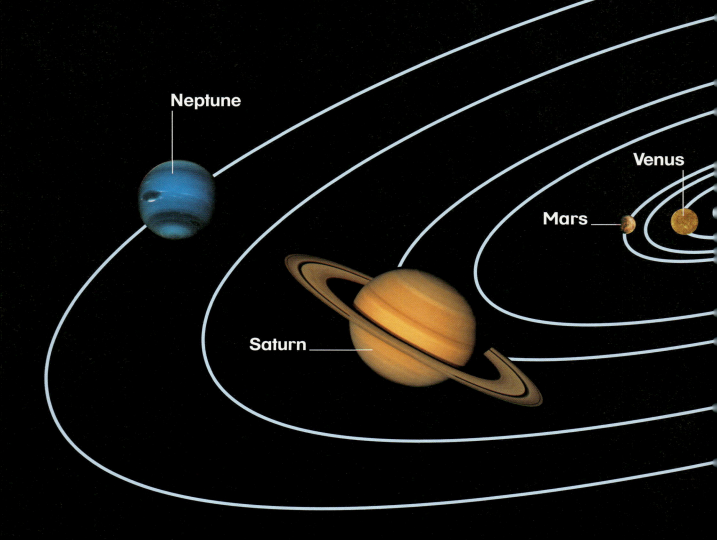

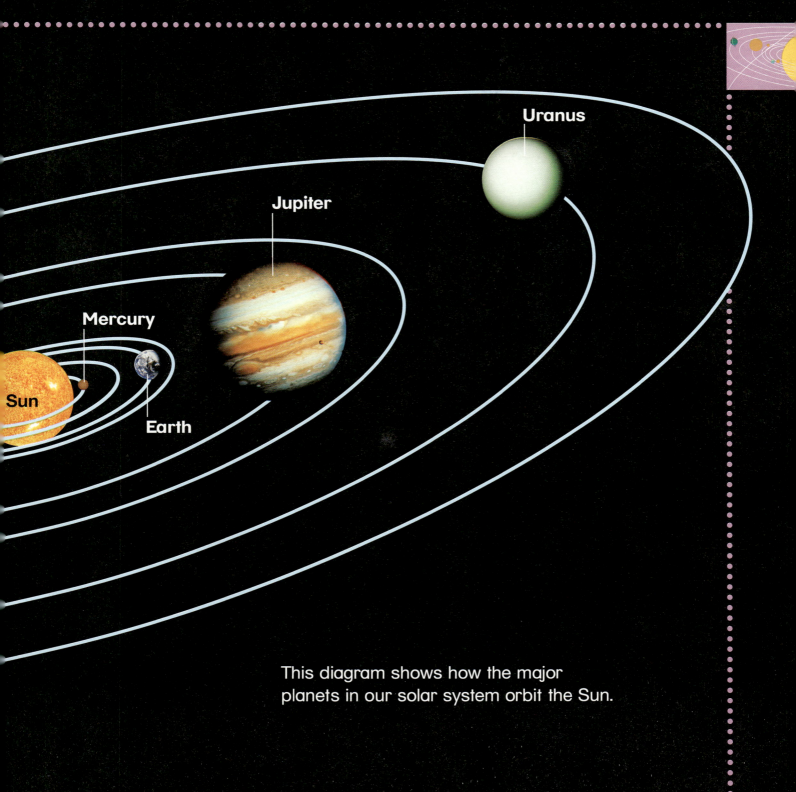

This diagram shows how the major planets in our solar system orbit the Sun.

Exploring Space

How do people explore space?

Long ago people explored space by looking at the night sky. Today scientists still do this, but they use telescopes to help them see more clearly. Astronauts and machines called space probes also explore space.

These telescopes on Mauna Kea, Hawaii, take pictures of space objects.

What do telescopes do?

People use telescopes to study space. Telescopes make distant objects appear larger and brighter. They allow people to see far into space more clearly. Some telescopes are used to take pictures of planets and stars.

Today scientists use computers to control most telescopes. Some telescopes are on Earth. Others, like the Hubble Space Telescope, are in space.

Hubble Space Telescope

What are space probes?

Space probes are machines that study space. The machines go to faraway planets and moons. Probes collect information and take close-up pictures that a telescope on Earth could not take.

One space probe scientists have used is called *Galileo*. The space probe took pictures of volcanoes erupting on one of Jupiter's moons. It sent the information and pictures back to scientists on Earth.

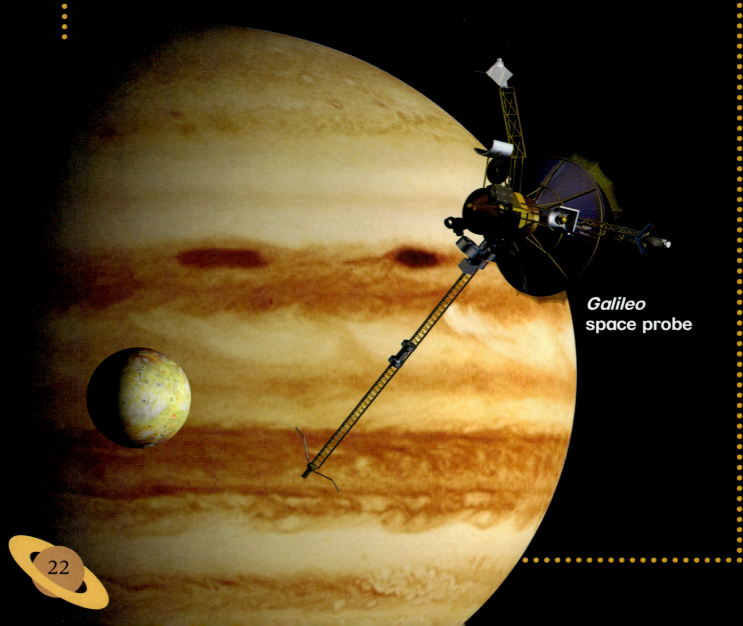

Galileo **space probe**

What do astronauts do?

Astronauts make new discoveries each time they travel into space. Sometimes they repair equipment in space. Some astronauts live aboard space stations. The experiments they carry out help others learn more about space and about Earth.

astronauts working in space

Key Events in Space Exploration

1957  *Sputnik I* is launched. It is the first object made by humans to orbit the Earth.

1959 *Luna 2* is the first spacecraft to land on the Moon.

1961 Cosmonaut Yuri Gagarin is the first person to travel in space. He journeys once around Earth on April 12, in a flight lasting 108 minutes.

1968 *Apollo 8* is the first spacecraft to fly with people around the Moon and return to Earth.

1969 On the *Apollo 11* mission, astronaut Neil Armstrong is the first person to walk on the Moon on July 20.

1981 The Space Shuttle *Columbia* was sent into orbit around Earth. It is the first spacecraft that could be reused in space.

1990 The Space Shuttle *Discovery* releases the Hubble Space Telescope. Its purpose is to study objects in space.

2000 The International Space Station opens in November. Astronauts and scientists from many nations live and work on the space station. They study what it is like to live in space.

Talk About It

1. What part of the book would you use to find information about the Moon?

2. Why is it important for scientists to study space?

3. What question do you have about space?

Word count: 1,065

DRA® Level	28
Guided Reading Level	M

Nonfiction Genre
Reference

Content Area
Earth Science

Comprehension Skill
Identify Text Organization and Structure

Nonfiction Features
Captions, Contents, Diagrams, Headings, Icons, Introduction, Italics, Labels, Scientific Illustrations, Star Diagrams, Tabbing Device, Time-Lapse Photographs, Timeline

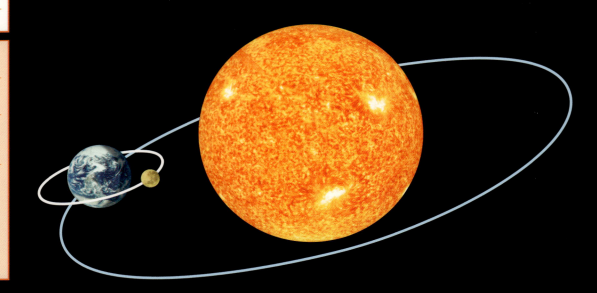

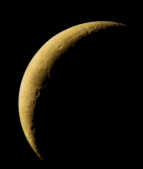

What makes a star shine? How far away is the Sun? *Book of Space* answers many questions you might ask about the Sun, Moon, stars, and solar system.

1-800-321-3106
www.pearsonlearning.com

ISBN 0-7652-5176-0

BOOK of SPACE
Questions and Answers

By Rosie McCormick

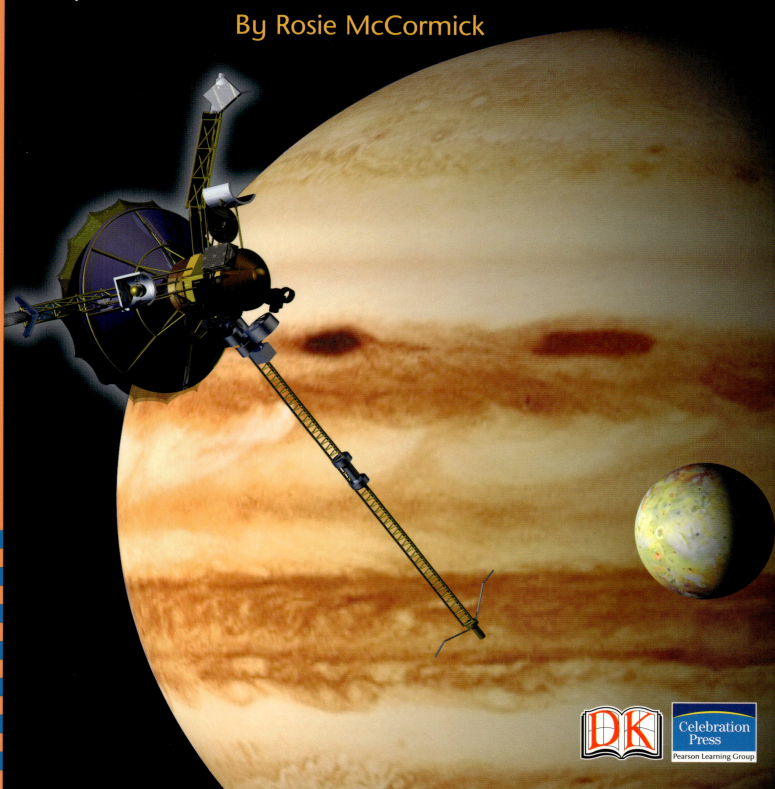

Program Development Consultant (K–2)
Nell Duke

The following people from **Pearson Learning Group**
have contributed to the development of this product:

Joan Mazzeo, Jennifer Visco **Design** | **Editorial** Lynn Trepicchio, Patricia D'Agostino
Christine Fleming **Marketing** | **Publishing Operations** Jennifer Van Der Heide
Production Laura Benford-Sullivan
Content Area Consultants Dr. Amy Rabb-Liu and Dr. Charles Liu

The following people from **DK** have
contributed to the development of this product:

Art Director Rachael Foster

Siân Williams, Jo Dixon, Georgina Ackroyd **Design** | **Managing Editor** Scarlett O'Hara
Brenda Clynch **Picture Research** | **Editorial** Elise See Tai
Richard Czapnik, Andy Smith **Cover Design** | **Production** Rosalind Holmes
Carole Stott **Consultant** | **DTP** David McDonald

Dorling Kindersley would like to thank: Andy Crawford for photography, Jo Dixon for original artwork, and Ross George for additional cover design work. Dorling Kindersley would also like to thank the following models for appearing in this book: Nathan Czapnik and Chloe Chetty.

Photographs: Every effort has been made to secure permission and provide appropriate credit for photographic material. The publisher deeply regrets any omission and pledges to correct errors called to its attention in subsequent editions.

Unless otherwise acknowledged, all photographs are the property of Dorling Kindersley

Photo locators denoted as follows: Top (T), Center (C), Bottom (B), Left (L), Right (R), Background (Bkgd)

Picture Credits: CVRL Stephen Girimont/Shutterstock; **001** NASA; **001** NASA; **003T** NASA; **004** Yuriy Mazur/Fotolia; **005** ESA/Hubble/NASA; **006** Bkgd pockygallery11/Fotolia; **006CR** D. A Gouliermis/ESA/Hubble/NASA; **007** Artur Synenko/Fotolia; **009** McCarthys/Fotolia; **010** siur/Fotolia; **012B** NASA; **013** NASA; **014** Vera Kuttelvaserova/Fotolia; **020** Christopher Bibbo/Fotolia; **022C** Stephen Girimont/Shutterstock; **023** NASA; **024** (1959) NASA; **024** (1961) NASA; **024** (1968) NASA; **024** (1981) NASA.

All other images: Dorling Kindersley © 2005. For further information see www.dkimages.com

Text Copyright © 2005 Pearson Education, Inc., publishing as Celebration Press, a division of Pearson Learning Group. Compilation Copyright © 2005 Dorling Kindersley Ltd. All rights reserved. No part of this book may be reproduced or transmitted in any form or by any means, electronic or mechanical, including photocopying, recording, or any information storage and retrieval system, without permission in writing from the proprietors.

For information regarding licensing and permissions, write to Rights and Permissions Department, Pearson Learning Group, 299 Jefferson Road, Parsippany, NJ 07054 USA or to Rights and Permissions Department, DK Publishing, The Penguin Group (UK), 80 Strand, London WC2R ORL.

ISBN: 0-7652-5176-0

Color reproduction by Colourscan, Singapore
Printed in Mexico
21 22 V0B4   15

1-800-321-3106
www.pearsonlearning.com

BOOK of SPACE
Questions and Answers

By Rosie McCormick

Contents

	Introduction	3
	Space	4
	Stars	6
	The Sun	10
	The Moon	12
	Our Solar System	16
	Exploring Space	20
	Key Events in Space Exploration	24

Introduction

What do you want to know about space?

People have always asked questions about space. You can find answers to some of your questions in this book. Scientists have found many answers to their questions by using telescopes, spacecraft, and other tools. They have made amazing discoveries, but there is still much more to explore.

Space

What makes up space?

When you look up at the night sky, you are looking at space. Space is filled with many things, including planets, moons, stars, and other objects. A star is a ball of gas that gives off light and heat. A planet is a large object that moves around a star. A moon is an object that moves around a planet.

What is our place in space?

We live on a planet called Earth. Earth moves around the Sun, which is a star. Many objects move around the Sun, including eight major planets. Earth is the third planet from the Sun.

Earth

Stars

What makes the stars shine?

Stars are huge balls of gas. They produce heat and light. Most stars look like bright dots because they are so far away. We cannot see their real colors. Very hot stars are blue. Medium-hot stars are yellow. The coolest stars are red.

The brightness of a star depends on how much light it produces. The hotter a star is, the more brightly it shines. Large stars are usually brighter than small stars. The closer a star is to Earth, the brighter it appears to us.

hot stars

Why do we only see most stars at night?

The Sun is the closest star to Earth. It is so close that it appears very bright. During the day the Sun is so bright that we usually cannot see other stars. Even though we cannot see the other stars and planets during the daytime, they are still in space.

What are constellations?

Sometimes people imagine that the stars form pictures in the sky. Sometimes they see the shapes of animals, objects, and people. Constellations are the groups of stars that form these pictures. Long ago some people gave the star pictures names such as the Lion, the Scorpion, and the Southern Cross. There are eighty-eight constellations that we can see in the entire sky.

Scorpion

Southern Cross

Lion

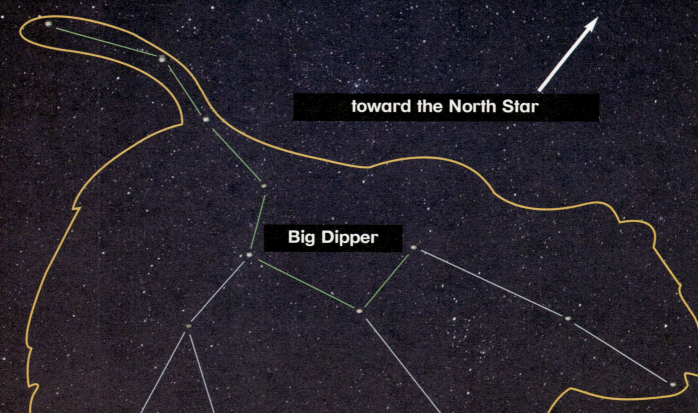

toward the North Star

Big Dipper

Big Bear

How do star watchers use constellations?

Star gazers use constellations to find individual stars. For example, one constellation is called the Big Bear. It contains a smaller group of seven stars called the Big Dipper. Two bright stars in the Big Dipper help you find the North Star. Sometimes when people are lost, they use the North Star to guide them.

The Sun

What kind of star is the Sun?

The Sun is a yellow star. The temperature of the center of the Sun is more than 25 million degrees Fahrenheit. For a star, that is only medium-hot. The Sun is much bigger than Earth. More than a million Earths could fit inside our Sun. Compared to other stars, however, the Sun is medium-sized.

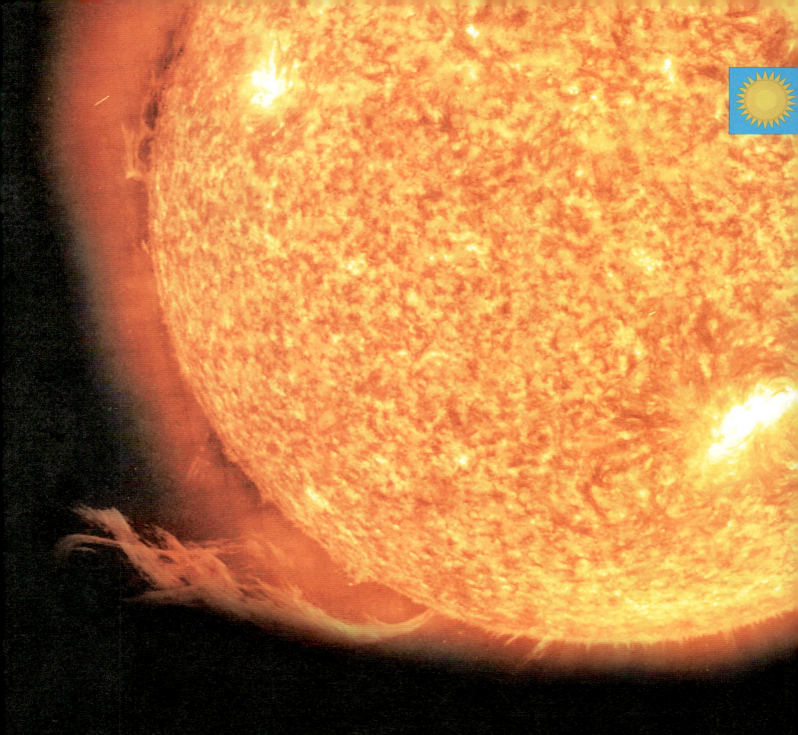

How far away is the Sun?

The Sun is about 93 million miles from Earth. If Earth were closer to the Sun, it would be too hot for people to live on our planet. If it were much farther away, it would be too cold.

The Moon

What is it like on the Moon?

The Moon is an object that moves around Earth. Like Earth, the Moon has rocks and soil. The surface of the Moon has many holes. These holes are called craters. There are also mountains on the Moon. On parts of the Moon the temperature is hotter than boiling water. On other parts it is colder than ice.

Can people live on the Moon?

People cannot live on the Moon today. Plants and animals need air to breathe and water to drink. There is no air or water on the Moon. To live on the Moon, people must bring air and water with them.

The craters on the Moon vary in size from less than an inch to many miles across.

How far away is the Moon?

The Moon is about 238,000 miles from Earth. If you could drive to the Moon, it would take months to get there. If you traveled by a spacecraft, it would take a few days. The Moon is our closest neighbor in space.

Moon

Earth

How does the Moon shine?

Even though the Moon shines, it has no light of its own. The light from the Moon comes from the Sun. The Sun shines on the Moon just like it shines on Earth. People see the part of the Moon that has the Sun's light shining on it.

Why does the Moon seem to change shape?

The Moon travels around Earth. As the Moon moves, only the surface that is lighted by the Sun can be seen on Earth. This makes it look like the Moon changes shape. The Moon does not change shape. It is always a sphere, like the shape of a ball.

full Moon

quarter Moon

crescent Moon

Our Solar System

What is our solar system?

Our solar system is made up of the Sun and the objects that move around it. There are eight major planets in our solar system. Many of them have moons. There are more than one hundred moons in all. There are also millions of smaller objects in our solar system such as asteroids and comets. Scientists discover new objects in our solar system all the time.

comet

What is an orbit?

An orbit is the path an object takes when it travels around something. When we say a planet "orbits" the Sun, we mean it follows a path around the Sun. All the planets in our solar system orbit the Sun. The Moon orbits Earth. Other moons orbit other planets.

What are the planets in our solar system?

The eight major planets in our solar system are Mercury, Venus, Earth, Mars, Jupiter, Saturn, Uranus, and Neptune. Mercury is the smallest and Jupiter is the biggest of these planets.

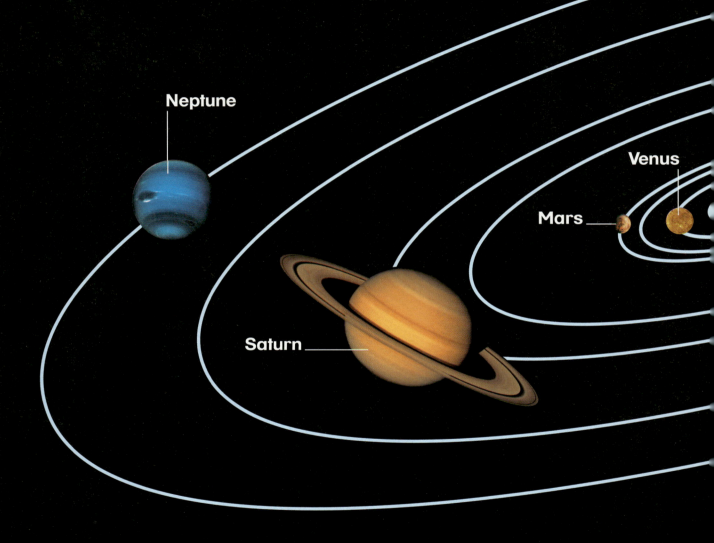

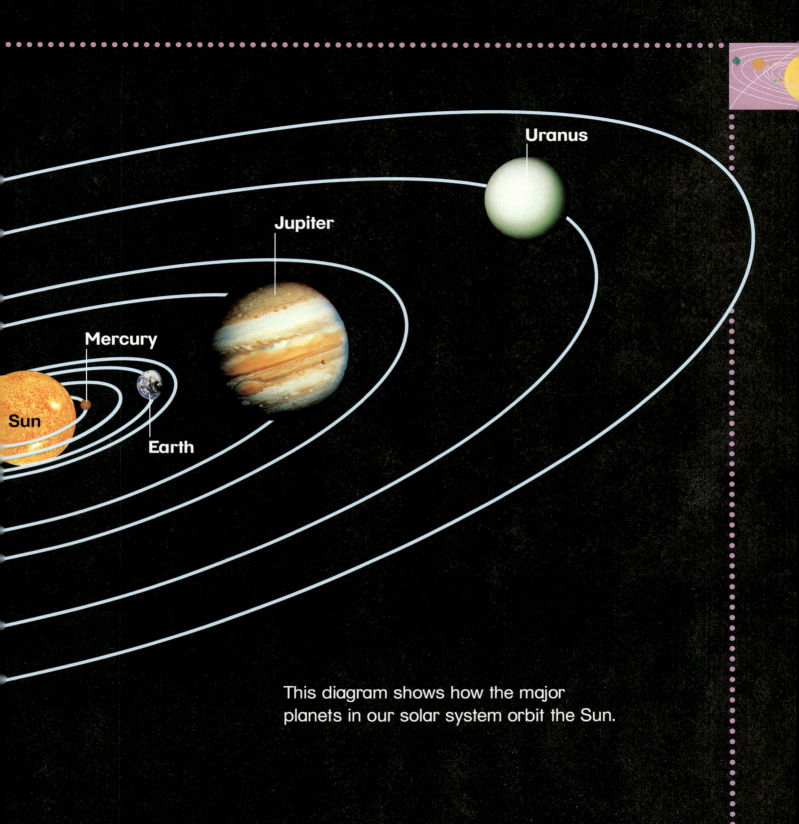

This diagram shows how the major planets in our solar system orbit the Sun.

Exploring Space

How do people explore space?

Long ago people explored space by looking at the night sky. Today scientists still do this, but they use telescopes to help them see more clearly. Astronauts and machines called space probes also explore space.

These telescopes on Mauna Kea, Hawaii, take pictures of space objects.

What do telescopes do?

People use telescopes to study space. Telescopes make distant objects appear larger and brighter. They allow people to see far into space more clearly. Some telescopes are used to take pictures of planets and stars.

Today scientists use computers to control most telescopes. Some telescopes are on Earth. Others, like the Hubble Space Telescope, are in space.

Hubble Space Telescope

What are space probes?

Space probes are machines that study space. The machines go to faraway planets and moons. Probes collect information and take close-up pictures that a telescope on Earth could not take.

One space probe scientists have used is called *Galileo*. The space probe took pictures of volcanoes erupting on one of Jupiter's moons. It sent the information and pictures back to scientists on Earth.

Galileo **space probe**

What do astronauts do?

Astronauts make new discoveries each time they travel into space. Sometimes they repair equipment in space. Some astronauts live aboard space stations. The experiments they carry out help others learn more about space and about Earth.

astronauts working in space

Key Events in Space Exploration

1957 *Sputnik I* is launched. It is the first object made by humans to orbit the Earth.

1959 *Luna 2* is the first spacecraft to land on the Moon.

1961 Cosmonaut Yuri Gagarin is the first person to travel in space. He journeys once around Earth on April 12, in a flight lasting 108 minutes.

1968 *Apollo 8* is the first spacecraft to fly with people around the Moon and return to Earth.

1969 On the *Apollo 11* mission, astronaut Neil Armstrong is the first person to walk on the Moon on July 20.

1981 The Space Shuttle *Columbia* was sent into orbit around Earth. It is the first spacecraft that could be reused in space.

1990 The Space Shuttle *Discovery* releases the Hubble Space Telescope. Its purpose is to study objects in space.

2000 The International Space Station opens in November. Astronauts and scientists from many nations live and work on the space station. They study what it is like to live in space.

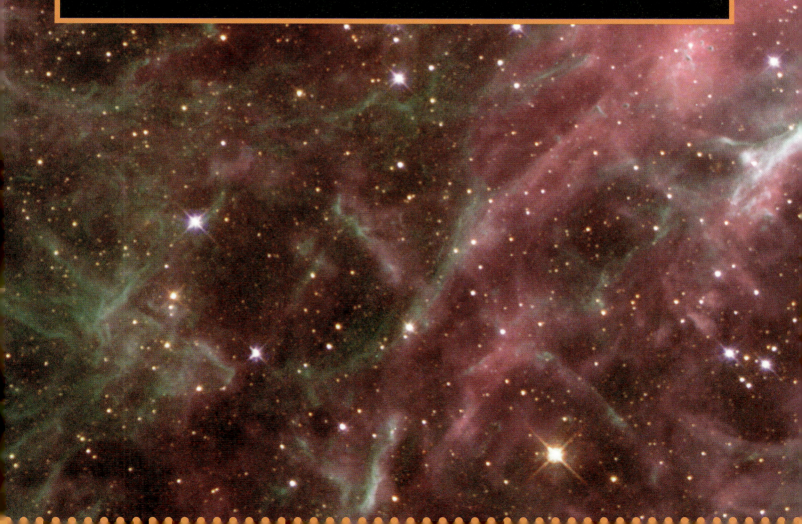

BOOK of SPACE
Questions and Answers

By Rosie McCormick

	Introduction	3
	Space	4
	Stars	6
	The Sun	10
	The Moon	12
	Our Solar System	16
	Exploring Space	20
	Key Events in Space Exploration	24

Introduction

What do you want to know about space?

People have always asked questions about space. You can find answers to some of your questions in this book. Scientists have found many answers to their questions by using telescopes, spacecraft, and other tools. They have made amazing discoveries, but there is still much more to explore.

Space

What makes up space?

When you look up at the night sky, you are looking at space. Space is filled with many things, including planets, moons, stars, and other objects. A star is a ball of gas that gives off light and heat. A planet is a large object that moves around a star. A moon is an object that moves around a planet.

What is our place in space?

We live on a planet called Earth. Earth moves around the Sun, which is a star. Many objects move around the Sun, including eight major planets. Earth is the third planet from the Sun.

Earth

Stars

What makes the stars shine?

Stars are huge balls of gas. They produce heat and light. Most stars look like bright dots because they are so far away. We cannot see their real colors. Very hot stars are blue. Medium-hot stars are yellow. The coolest stars are red.

The brightness of a star depends on how much light it produces. The hotter a star is, the more brightly it shines. Large stars are usually brighter than small stars. The closer a star is to Earth, the brighter it appears to us.

hot stars

Why do we only see most stars at night?

The Sun is the closest star to Earth. It is so close that it appears very bright. During the day the Sun is so bright that we usually cannot see other stars. Even though we cannot see the other stars and planets during the daytime, they are still in space.

What are constellations?

Sometimes people imagine that the stars form pictures in the sky. Sometimes they see the shapes of animals, objects, and people. Constellations are the groups of stars that form these pictures. Long ago some people gave the star pictures names such as the Lion, the Scorpion, and the Southern Cross. There are eighty-eight constellations that we can see in the entire sky.

Scorpion

Southern Cross

Lion

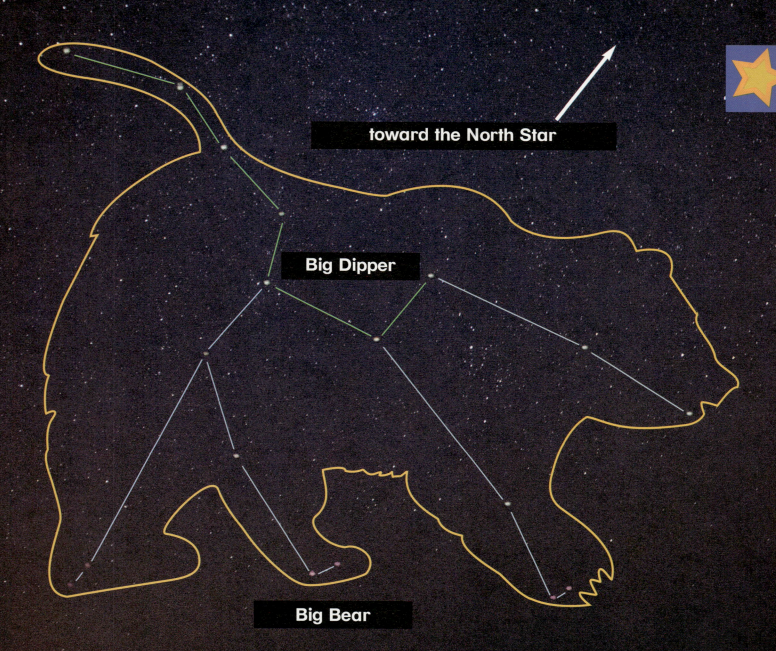

toward the North Star

Big Dipper

Big Bear

How do star watchers use constellations?

Star gazers use constellations to find individual stars. For example, one constellation is called the Big Bear. It contains a smaller group of seven stars called the Big Dipper. Two bright stars in the Big Dipper help you find the North Star. Sometimes when people are lost, they use the North Star to guide them.

The Sun

What kind of star is the Sun?

The Sun is a yellow star. The temperature of the center of the Sun is more than 25 million degrees Fahrenheit. For a star, that is only medium-hot. The Sun is much bigger than Earth. More than a million Earths could fit inside our Sun. Compared to other stars, however, the Sun is medium-sized.

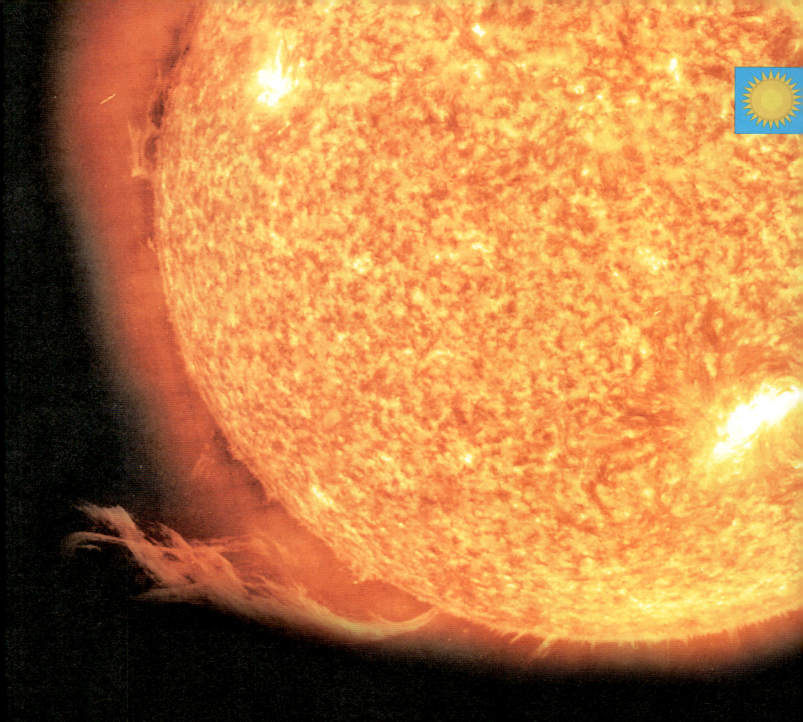

How far away is the Sun?

The Sun is about 93 million miles from Earth. If Earth were closer to the Sun, it would be too hot for people to live on our planet. If it were much farther away, it would be too cold.

The Moon

What is it like on the Moon?

The Moon is an object that moves around Earth. Like Earth, the Moon has rocks and soil. The surface of the Moon has many holes. These holes are called craters. There are also mountains on the Moon. On parts of the Moon the temperature is hotter than boiling water. On other parts it is colder than ice.

Can people live on the Moon?

People cannot live on the Moon today. Plants and animals need air to breathe and water to drink. There is no air or water on the Moon. To live on the Moon, people must bring air and water with them.

The craters on the Moon vary in size from less than an inch to many miles across.

How far away is the Moon?

The Moon is about 238,000 miles from Earth. If you could drive to the Moon, it would take months to get there. If you traveled by a spacecraft, it would take a few days. The Moon is our closest neighbor in space.

Moon

Earth

How does the Moon shine?

Even though the Moon shines, it has no light of its own. The light from the Moon comes from the Sun. The Sun shines on the Moon just like it shines on Earth. People see the part of the Moon that has the Sun's light shining on it.

Why does the Moon seem to change shape?

The Moon travels around Earth. As the Moon moves, only the surface that is lighted by the Sun can be seen on Earth. This makes it look like the Moon changes shape. The Moon does not change shape. It is always a sphere, like the shape of a ball.

full Moon

quarter Moon

crescent Moon

Our Solar System

What is our solar system?

Our solar system is made up of the Sun and the objects that move around it. There are eight major planets in our solar system. Many of them have moons. There are more than one hundred moons in all. There are also millions of smaller objects in our solar system such as asteroids and comets. Scientists discover new objects in our solar system all the time.

comet

What is an orbit?

An orbit is the path an object takes when it travels around something. When we say a planet "orbits" the Sun, we mean it follows a path around the Sun. All the planets in our solar system orbit the Sun. The Moon orbits Earth. Other moons orbit other planets.

asteroid

What are the planets in our solar system?

The eight major planets in our solar system are Mercury, Venus, Earth, Mars, Jupiter, Saturn, Uranus, and Neptune. Mercury is the smallest and Jupiter is the biggest of these planets.

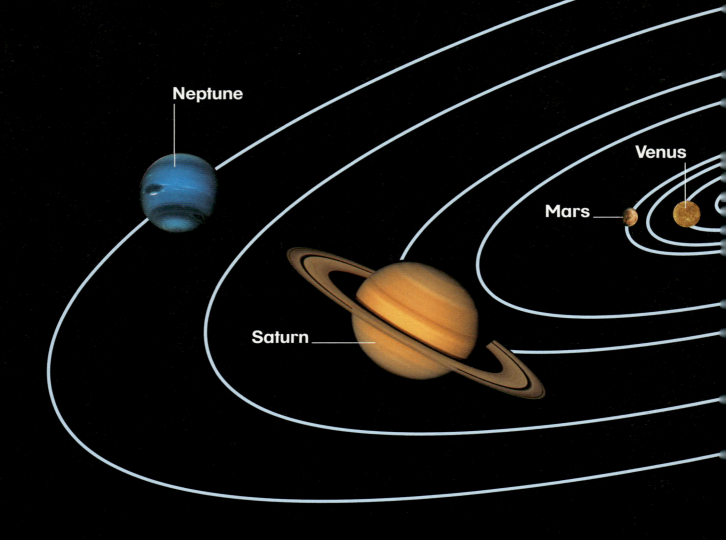

This diagram shows how the major planets in our solar system orbit the Sun.

Exploring Space

How do people explore space?

Long ago people explored space by looking at the night sky. Today scientists still do this, but they use telescopes to help them see more clearly. Astronauts and machines called space probes also explore space.

These telescopes on Mauna Kea, Hawaii, take pictures of space objects.

What do telescopes do?

People use telescopes to study space. Telescopes make distant objects appear larger and brighter. They allow people to see far into space more clearly. Some telescopes are used to take pictures of planets and stars.

Today scientists use computers to control most telescopes. Some telescopes are on Earth. Others, like the Hubble Space Telescope, are in space.

Hubble Space Telescope

What are space probes?

Space probes are machines that study space. The machines go to faraway planets and moons. Probes collect information and take close-up pictures that a telescope on Earth could not take.

One space probe scientists have used is called *Galileo*. The space probe took pictures of volcanoes erupting on one of Jupiter's moons. It sent the information and pictures back to scientists on Earth.

Galileo **space probe**

What do astronauts do?

Astronauts make new discoveries each time they travel into space. Sometimes they repair equipment in space. Some astronauts live aboard space stations. The experiments they carry out help others learn more about space and about Earth.

astronauts working in space

Key Events in Space Exploration

1957  *Sputnik I* is launched. It is the first object made by humans to orbit the Earth.

1959 *Luna 2* is the first spacecraft to land on the Moon.

1961 Cosmonaut Yuri Gagarin is the first person to travel in space. He journeys once around Earth on April 12, in a flight lasting 108 minutes.

1968 *Apollo 8* is the first spacecraft to fly with people around the Moon and return to Earth.

1969 On the *Apollo 11* mission, astronaut Neil Armstrong is the first person to walk on the Moon on July 20.

1981 The Space Shuttle *Columbia* was sent into orbit around Earth. It is the first spacecraft that could be reused in space.

1990 The Space Shuttle *Discovery* releases the Hubble Space Telescope. Its purpose is to study objects in space.

2000 The International Space Station opens in November. Astronauts and scientists from many nations live and work on the space station. They study what it is like to live in space.

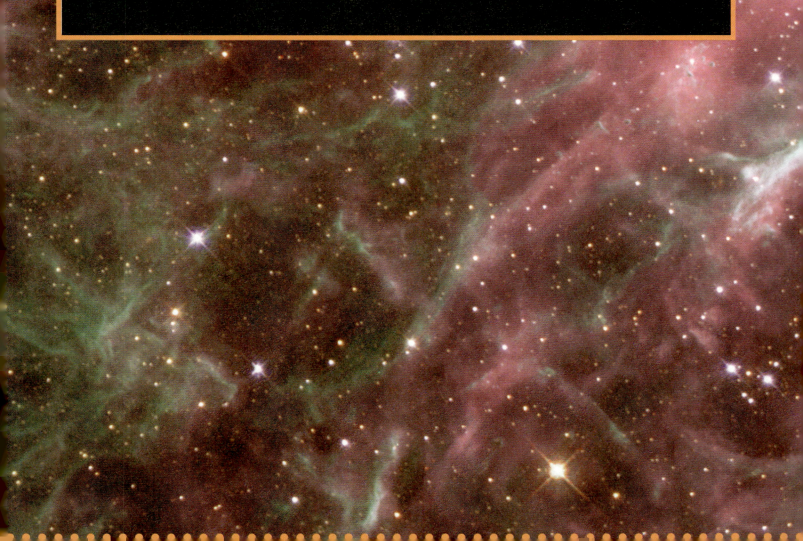

BOOK of SPACE
Questions and Answers

By Rosie McCormick

Contents

Introduction — 3

Space — 4

Stars — 6

The Sun — 10

The Moon — 12

Our Solar System — 16

Exploring Space — 20

Key Events in Space Exploration — 24

Introduction

What do you want to know about space?

People have always asked questions about space. You can find answers to some of your questions in this book. Scientists have found many answers to their questions by using telescopes, spacecraft, and other tools. They have made amazing discoveries, but there is still much more to explore.

Space

What makes up space?

When you look up at the night sky, you are looking at space. Space is filled with many things, including planets, moons, stars, and other objects. A star is a ball of gas that gives off light and heat. A planet is a large object that moves around a star. A moon is an object that moves around a planet.

What is our place in space?

We live on a planet called Earth. Earth moves around the Sun, which is a star. Many objects move around the Sun, including eight major planets. Earth is the third planet from the Sun.

Earth

Stars

What makes the stars shine?

Stars are huge balls of gas. They produce heat and light. Most stars look like bright dots because they are so far away. We cannot see their real colors. Very hot stars are blue. Medium-hot stars are yellow. The coolest stars are red.

The brightness of a star depends on how much light it produces. The hotter a star is, the more brightly it shines. Large stars are usually brighter than small stars. The closer a star is to Earth, the brighter it appears to us.

hot stars

Why do we only see most stars at night?

The Sun is the closest star to Earth. It is so close that it appears very bright. During the day the Sun is so bright that we usually cannot see other stars. Even though we cannot see the other stars and planets during the daytime, they are still in space.

What are constellations?

Sometimes people imagine that the stars form pictures in the sky. Sometimes they see the shapes of animals, objects, and people. Constellations are the groups of stars that form these pictures. Long ago some people gave the star pictures names such as the Lion, the Scorpion, and the Southern Cross. There are eighty-eight constellations that we can see in the entire sky.

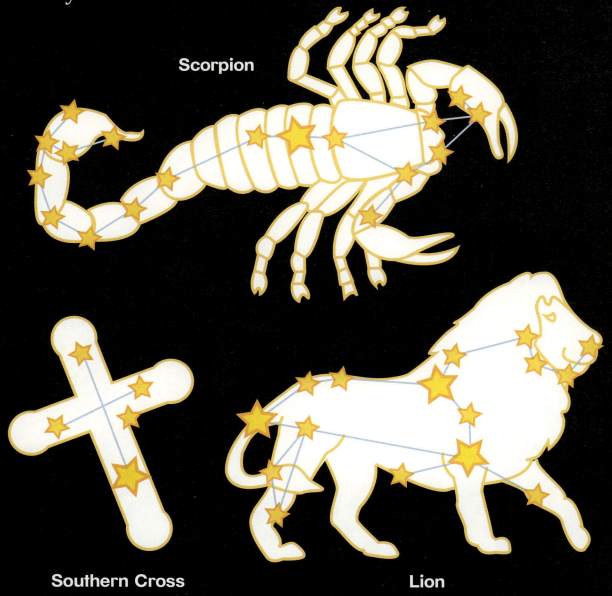

Scorpion

Southern Cross

Lion

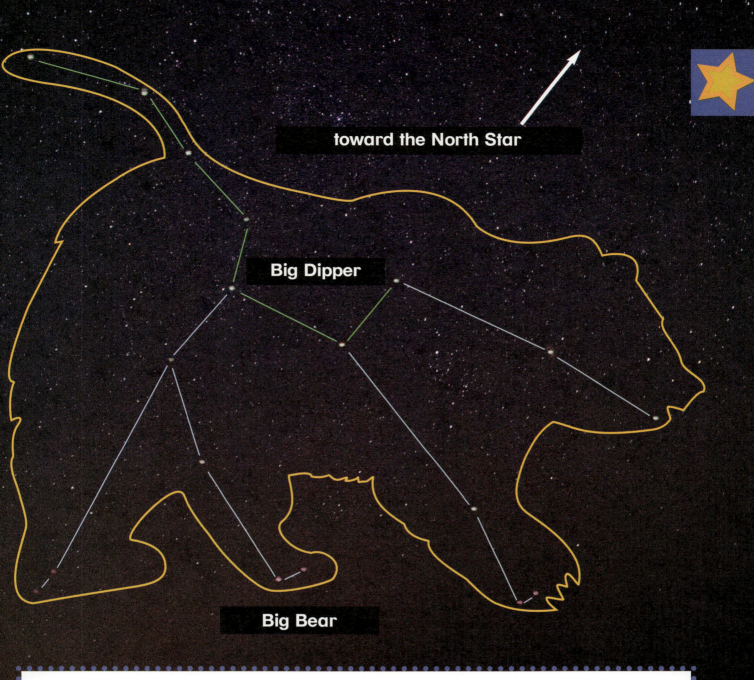

How do star watchers use constellations?

Star gazers use constellations to find individual stars. For example, one constellation is called the Big Bear. It contains a smaller group of seven stars called the Big Dipper. Two bright stars in the Big Dipper help you find the North Star. Sometimes when people are lost, they use the North Star to guide them.

The Sun

What kind of star is the Sun?

The Sun is a yellow star. The temperature of the center of the Sun is more than 25 million degrees Fahrenheit. For a star, that is only medium-hot. The Sun is much bigger than Earth. More than a million Earths could fit inside our Sun. Compared to other stars, however, the Sun is medium-sized.

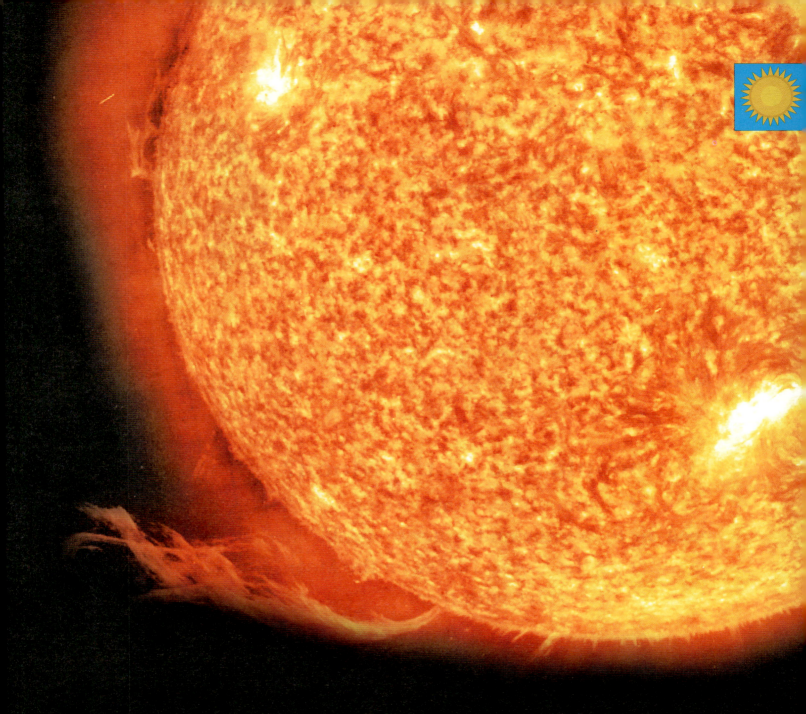

How far away is the Sun?

The Sun is about 93 million miles from Earth. If Earth were closer to the Sun, it would be too hot for people to live on our planet. If it were much farther away, it would be too cold.

The Moon

What is it like on the Moon?

The Moon is an object that moves around Earth. Like Earth, the Moon has rocks and soil. The surface of the Moon has many holes. These holes are called craters. There are also mountains on the Moon. On parts of the Moon the temperature is hotter than boiling water. On other parts it is colder than ice.

Can people live on the Moon?

People cannot live on the Moon today. Plants and animals need air to breathe and water to drink. There is no air or water on the Moon. To live on the Moon, people must bring air and water with them.

The craters on the Moon vary in size from less than an inch to many miles across.

How far away is the Moon?

The Moon is about 238,000 miles from Earth. If you could drive to the Moon, it would take months to get there. If you traveled by a spacecraft, it would take a few days. The Moon is our closest neighbor in space.

Moon

Earth

How does the Moon shine?

Even though the Moon shines, it has no light of its own. The light from the Moon comes from the Sun. The Sun shines on the Moon just like it shines on Earth. People see the part of the Moon that has the Sun's light shining on it.

Why does the Moon seem to change shape?

The Moon travels around Earth. As the Moon moves, only the surface that is lighted by the Sun can be seen on Earth. This makes it look like the Moon changes shape. The Moon does not change shape. It is always a sphere, like the shape of a ball.

full Moon

quarter Moon

crescent Moon

Our Solar System

What is our solar system?

Our solar system is made up of the Sun and the objects that move around it. There are eight major planets in our solar system. Many of them have moons. There are more than one hundred moons in all. There are also millions of smaller objects in our solar system such as asteroids and comets. Scientists discover new objects in our solar system all the time.

comet

What is an orbit?

An orbit is the path an object takes when it travels around something. When we say a planet "orbits" the Sun, we mean it follows a path around the Sun. All the planets in our solar system orbit the Sun. The Moon orbits Earth. Other moons orbit other planets.

Earth

Sun

Moon

asteroid

What are the planets in our solar system?

The eight major planets in our solar system are Mercury, Venus, Earth, Mars, Jupiter, Saturn, Uranus, and Neptune. Mercury is the smallest and Jupiter is the biggest of these planets.

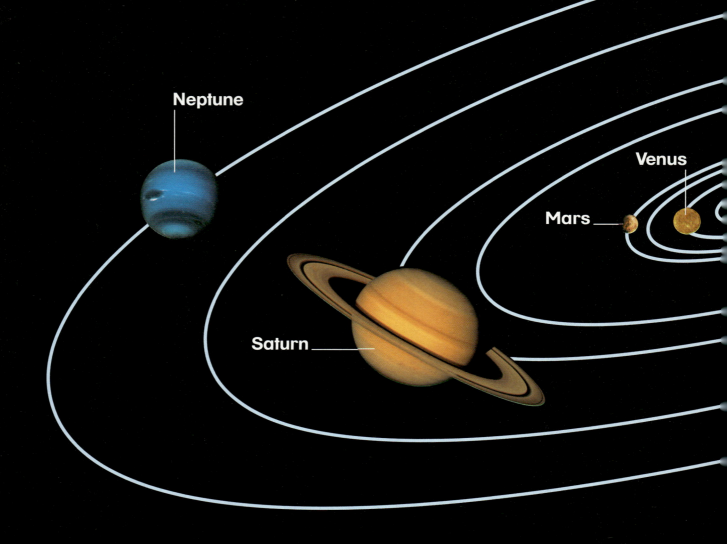

This diagram shows how the major planets in our solar system orbit the Sun.

Exploring Space

How do people explore space?

Long ago people explored space by looking at the night sky. Today scientists still do this, but they use telescopes to help them see more clearly. Astronauts and machines called space probes also explore space.

These telescopes on Mauna Kea, Hawaii, take pictures of space objects.

What do telescopes do?

People use telescopes to study space. Telescopes make distant objects appear larger and brighter. They allow people to see far into space more clearly. Some telescopes are used to take pictures of planets and stars.

Today scientists use computers to control most telescopes. Some telescopes are on Earth. Others, like the Hubble Space Telescope, are in space.

Hubble Space Telescope

What are space probes?

Space probes are machines that study space. The machines go to faraway planets and moons. Probes collect information and take close-up pictures that a telescope on Earth could not take.

One space probe scientists have used is called *Galileo*. The space probe took pictures of volcanoes erupting on one of Jupiter's moons. It sent the information and pictures back to scientists on Earth.

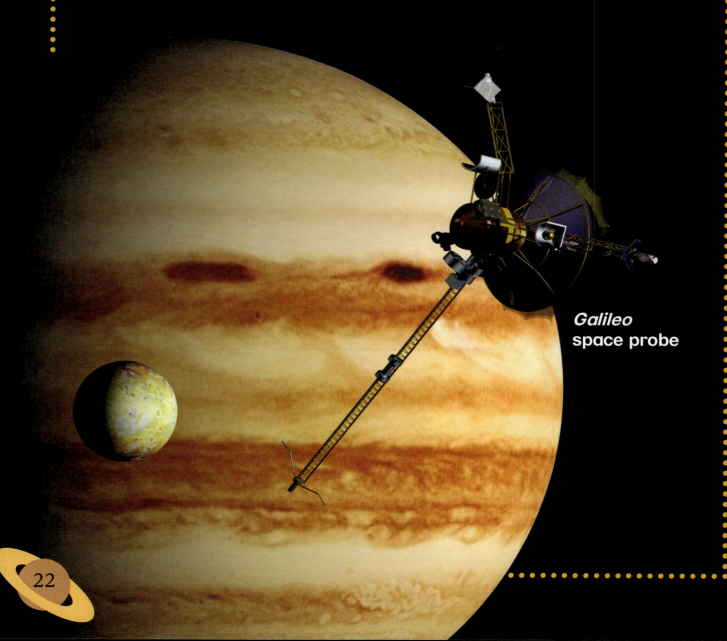

Galileo
space probe

What do astronauts do?

Astronauts make new discoveries each time they travel into space. Sometimes they repair equipment in space. Some astronauts live aboard space stations. The experiments they carry out help others learn more about space and about Earth.

astronauts working in space

Key Events in Space Exploration

1957 *Sputnik 1* is launched. It is the first object made by humans to orbit the Earth.

1959 *Luna 2* is the first spacecraft to land on the Moon.

1961 Cosmonaut Yuri Gagarin is the first person to travel in space. He journeys once around Earth on April 12, in a flight lasting 108 minutes.

1968 *Apollo 8* is the first spacecraft to fly with people around the Moon and return to Earth.

1969 On the *Apollo 11* mission, astronaut Neil Armstrong is the first person to walk on the Moon on July 20.

1981 The Space Shuttle *Columbia* was sent into orbit around Earth. It is the first spacecraft that could be reused in space.

1990 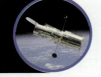 The Space Shuttle *Discovery* releases the Hubble Space Telescope. Its purpose is to study objects in space.

2000 The International Space Station opens in November. Astronauts and scientists from many nations live and work on the space station. They study what it is like to live in space.

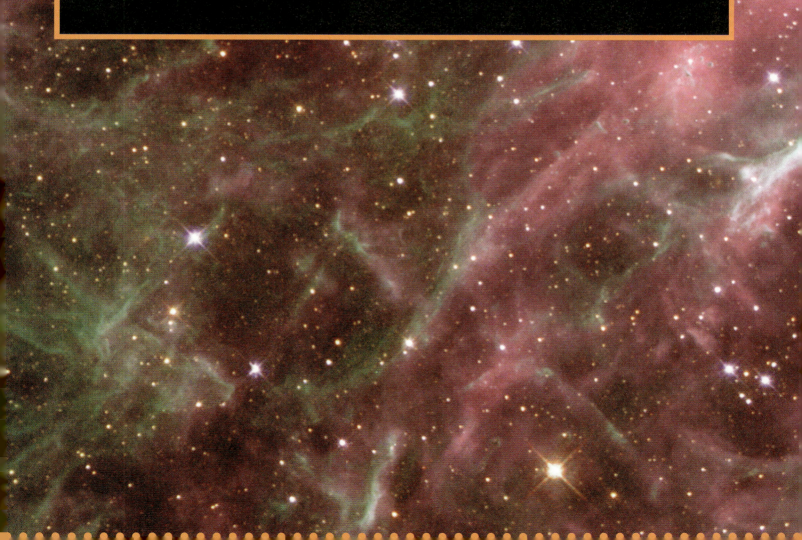

BOOK of SPACE
Questions and Answers

By Rosie McCormick

Contents

	Introduction	3
	Space	4
	Stars	6
	The Sun	10
	The Moon	12
	Our Solar System	16
	Exploring Space	20
	Key Events in Space Exploration	24

Introduction

What do you want to know about space?

People have always asked questions about space. You can find answers to some of your questions in this book. Scientists have found many answers to their questions by using telescopes, spacecraft, and other tools. They have made amazing discoveries, but there is still much more to explore.

Space

What makes up space?

When you look up at the night sky, you are looking at space. Space is filled with many things, including planets, moons, stars, and other objects. A star is a ball of gas that gives off light and heat. A planet is a large object that moves around a star. A moon is an object that moves around a planet.

What is our place in space?

We live on a planet called Earth. Earth moves around the Sun, which is a star. Many objects move around the Sun, including eight major planets. Earth is the third planet from the Sun.

Earth

Stars

What makes the stars shine?

Stars are huge balls of gas. They produce heat and light. Most stars look like bright dots because they are so far away. We cannot see their real colors. Very hot stars are blue. Medium-hot stars are yellow. The coolest stars are red.

The brightness of a star depends on how much light it produces. The hotter a star is, the more brightly it shines. Large stars are usually brighter than small stars. The closer a star is to Earth, the brighter it appears to us.

hot stars

Why do we only see most stars at night?

The Sun is the closest star to Earth. It is so close that it appears very bright. During the day the Sun is so bright that we usually cannot see other stars. Even though we cannot see the other stars and planets during the daytime, they are still in space.

What are constellations?

Sometimes people imagine that the stars form pictures in the sky. Sometimes they see the shapes of animals, objects, and people. Constellations are the groups of stars that form these pictures. Long ago some people gave the star pictures names such as the Lion, the Scorpion, and the Southern Cross. There are eighty-eight constellations that we can see in the entire sky.

Scorpion

Southern Cross

Lion

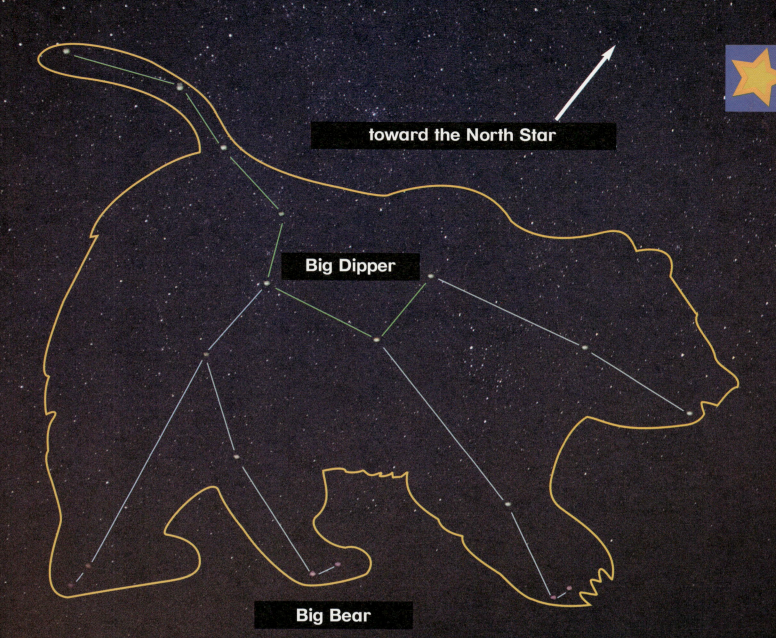

How do star watchers use constellations?

Star gazers use constellations to find individual stars. For example, one constellation is called the Big Bear. It contains a smaller group of seven stars called the Big Dipper. Two bright stars in the Big Dipper help you find the North Star. Sometimes when people are lost, they use the North Star to guide them.

The Sun

What kind of star is the Sun?

The Sun is a yellow star. The temperature of the center of the Sun is more than 25 million degrees Fahrenheit. For a star, that is only medium-hot. The Sun is much bigger than Earth. More than a million Earths could fit inside our Sun. Compared to other stars, however, the Sun is medium-sized.

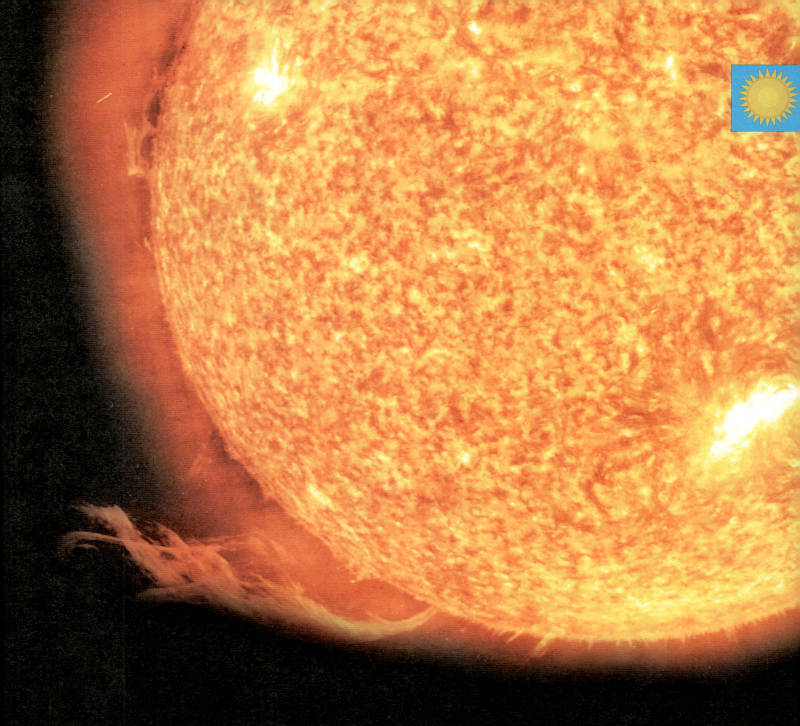

How far away is the Sun?

The Sun is about 93 million miles from Earth. If Earth were closer to the Sun, it would be too hot for people to live on our planet. If it were much farther away, it would be too cold.

The Moon

What is it like on the Moon?

The Moon is an object that moves around Earth. Like Earth, the Moon has rocks and soil. The surface of the Moon has many holes. These holes are called craters. There are also mountains on the Moon. On parts of the Moon the temperature is hotter than boiling water. On other parts it is colder than ice.

Can people live on the Moon?

People cannot live on the Moon today. Plants and animals need air to breathe and water to drink. There is no air or water on the Moon. To live on the Moon, people must bring air and water with them.

The craters on the Moon vary in size from less than an inch to many miles across.

How far away is the Moon?

The Moon is about 238,000 miles from Earth. If you could drive to the Moon, it would take months to get there. If you traveled by a spacecraft, it would take a few days. The Moon is our closest neighbor in space.

Moon

Earth

How does the Moon shine?

Even though the Moon shines, it has no light of its own. The light from the Moon comes from the Sun. The Sun shines on the Moon just like it shines on Earth. People see the part of the Moon that has the Sun's light shining on it.

Why does the Moon seem to change shape?

The Moon travels around Earth. As the Moon moves, only the surface that is lighted by the Sun can be seen on Earth. This makes it look like the Moon changes shape. The Moon does not change shape. It is always a sphere, like the shape of a ball.

full Moon

quarter Moon

crescent Moon

Our Solar System

What is our solar system?

Our solar system is made up of the Sun and the objects that move around it. There are eight major planets in our solar system. Many of them have moons. There are more than one hundred moons in all. There are also millions of smaller objects in our solar system such as asteroids and comets. Scientists discover new objects in our solar system all the time.

comet

What is an orbit?

An orbit is the path an object takes when it travels around something. When we say a planet "orbits" the Sun, we mean it follows a path around the Sun. All the planets in our solar system orbit the Sun. The Moon orbits Earth. Other moons orbit other planets.

Earth

Sun

Moon

asteroid

What are the planets in our solar system?

The eight major planets in our solar system are Mercury, Venus, Earth, Mars, Jupiter, Saturn, Uranus, and Neptune. Mercury is the smallest and Jupiter is the biggest of these planets.

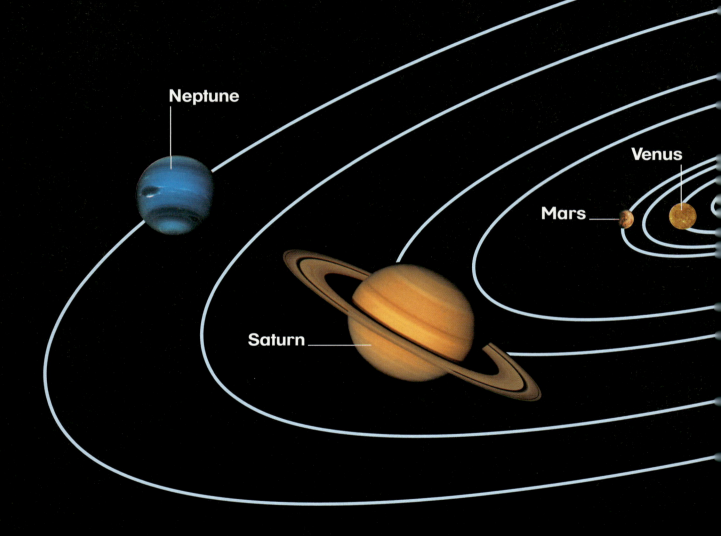

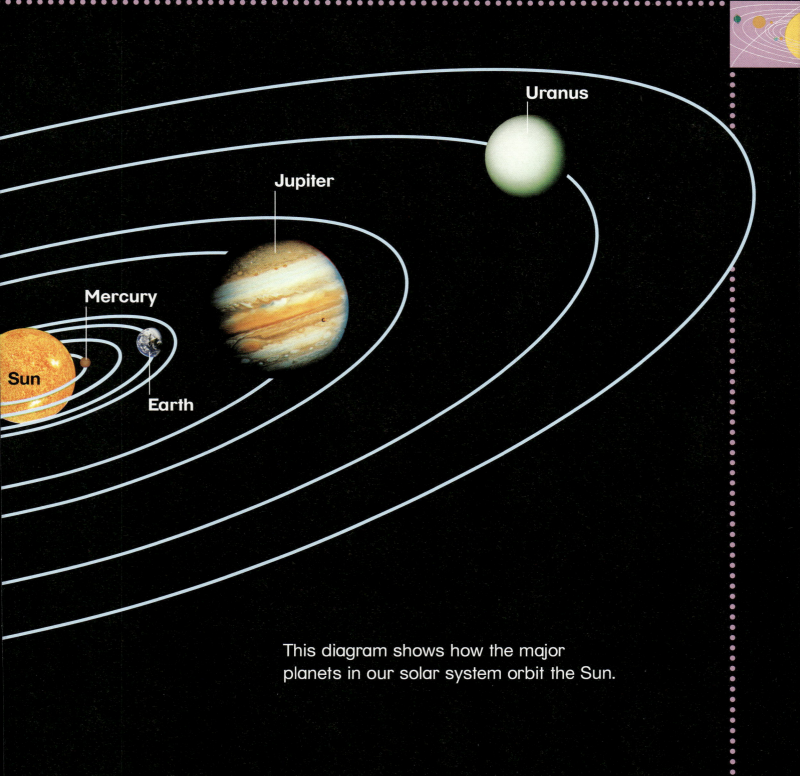

This diagram shows how the major planets in our solar system orbit the Sun.

Exploring Space

How do people explore space?

Long ago people explored space by looking at the night sky. Today scientists still do this, but they use telescopes to help them see more clearly. Astronauts and machines called space probes also explore space.

These telescopes on Mauna Kea, Hawaii, take pictures of space objects.

What do telescopes do?

People use telescopes to study space. Telescopes make distant objects appear larger and brighter. They allow people to see far into space more clearly. Some telescopes are used to take pictures of planets and stars.

Today scientists use computers to control most telescopes. Some telescopes are on Earth. Others, like the Hubble Space Telescope, are in space.

Hubble Space Telescope

What are space probes?

Space probes are machines that study space. The machines go to faraway planets and moons. Probes collect information and take close-up pictures that a telescope on Earth could not take.

One space probe scientists have used is called *Galileo*. The space probe took pictures of volcanoes erupting on one of Jupiter's moons. It sent the information and pictures back to scientists on Earth.

Galileo **space probe**

What do astronauts do?

Astronauts make new discoveries each time they travel into space. Sometimes they repair equipment in space. Some astronauts live aboard space stations. The experiments they carry out help others learn more about space and about Earth.

astronauts working in space

Key Events in Space Exploration

1957 *Sputnik I* is launched. It is the first object made by humans to orbit the Earth.

1959 *Luna 2* is the first spacecraft to land on the Moon.

1961 Cosmonaut Yuri Gagarin is the first person to travel in space. He journeys once around Earth on April 12, in a flight lasting 108 minutes.

1968 *Apollo 8* is the first spacecraft to fly with people around the Moon and return to Earth.

1969 On the *Apollo 11* mission, astronaut Neil Armstrong is the first person to walk on the Moon on July 20.

1981 The Space Shuttle *Columbia* was sent into orbit around Earth. It is the first spacecraft that could be reused in space.

1990 The Space Shuttle *Discovery* releases the Hubble Space Telescope. Its purpose is to study objects in space.

2000 The International Space Station opens in November. Astronauts and scientists from many nations live and work on the space station. They study what it is like to live in space.